RELEASED
TO
HEALING

RELEASED
TO
HEALING

Pages from my personal journal

Patrice Brown

Released to Healing
Pages from My Personal Journal

My Why?

Have you ever been in a place where you know, without a shadow of a doubt, God is speaking directly to you? Have you ever prayed about a situation and finally God's answer comes, and you know you must move? That was me on October 31, 2020, amid COVID-19. My life changed as a result of me tuning in to Him and moving on His command.

I suffered from low self-esteem for a long time. I could always mask it well. I was taught early to put on a smile and never let anyone know what was really going on. I had become an introvert to shield and protect myself from people getting too close to me because the closer someone got, the more I feared they would figure out what was really going on in my household, my life, and my head. I lived a life of fear, hopelessness. doubt, unworthiness, hurt, anger, self-hate, self-pity, jealousy, and depression.

On October 31, 2020, I got a word from the Lord. That word was "Released!" When I got it, I instantaneously felt a shifting, as if weight was coming off me. I had prayed about situations going on in my life...and with one word from the Lord, it began to shift.

Please don't think it was an easy journey for me, and don't think the journey is over. This book is about the process. This book contains my actual personal journal entries during one of the most difficult yet rewarding times of my life.

Why share my personal journal?
I do not believe God allows us to make it through trials for us to keep it to ourselves. We all know trials come to make us strong, but they are also testimonies designed for the building of the Kingdom. If you don't know how to journal, maybe this will help. If you don't know how to have a relationship with God, maybe this will help. If you are afraid to move on the word God has given you, maybe this will help. If you are afraid to speak up because you think someone will judge, maybe this will help. If you don't know where to start...this will help.

Introduction

Today is June 3rd, 2023, and a couple of days ago three exactly, I was going through some of my old journals looking for something and I started reading one journal. I knew that God had given me the word "release" one day during Covid and I moved on it. After that day, my life totally changed.

As I looked through the journal, I discovered I had written in it on that exact day. As I started reading the pages that followed, I began crying. I cried because God's Word was proven true again in my life. He has yet to fail me. I cried because it reminded me of where I was and how far I had come. I cried because I was overwhelmed with my process and progress towards my healing. I cried because, had I not listened to God at that specific time, I would not know Him as I do in this moment. I would not (no way, no how), be able to share this. I cried because I came to realize that my healing began at the time I obeyed.

As I read, I remembered specific things I was going through, and feelings I had during those moments. I know God was with me all the way. Every day was not perfect, by no means. Did I slip up? Yes. But I quickly fell to my knees. And He stayed with me the entire time. He provided for me when I didn't know where provision was coming from. He was faithful to His word.

Because I trusted Him, He did everything else. He would do exceedingly and abundantly more than I could ever ask or think. He would fight every battle. I trusted him. And I have been healing ever since.

I come from an abusive household. I ended up in abusive relationships. Both me and the other parties played our roles. I had six pregnancies with my second husband, and four children born from those six pregnancies after being told that I would never have children (2 miscarriages). Prior to hearing release, I lived in a state of fear. If you saw me, you would never know. I wore a smile, and I wore it perfectly.

I wouldn't drive at night. I was afraid.
I didn't like long road trips. I was afraid.
I would never even think about traveling by myself, I was afraid.
I wouldn't take an Expressway in Florida because it went up too high, I was afraid.
I wouldn't speak up about things I knew were incorrect when it came to God's word, I was afraid.

I always wanted to please man. That's what I thought I was supposed to do. Just go along with it. Don't question. Or if you question...No, I was afraid. I couldn't even think about talking about what was happening in my household, or in my past, or when I was a child. I was afraid.
What would people think? What would they say? How would they look at me? I wasn't good

enough. They wouldn't want to be my friend. Would they say I wasn't a Christian? Would they judge me? Would they say I didn't know how to pray effectively? Would they judge my parents? Would they see me as less than? Would they reject me? My life was not perfect, (you know how people paint a perfect picture) so would I be the outcast? They (other people I saw or thought were friends) appeared to be perfect, so I had to be too. All the while in my appearance of perfection, I was dying on the inside. Satan had me bound. Tied up, chained up, in quicksand, sinking quicker and quicker.

When the word release came, I didn't understand all that God would release me from. God released me from an imprisoned mindset. I had put so much value in what satan said to me about me that it drowned out everything God said. I could and would boldly speak the word of God to others about who God called them to be, but I didn't believe it for myself. My mind was in shackles. That one-word "release" freed me. And it allowed me to begin a process of healing.

This book is not to boast about anything that I am or anything that I've done, because I am nobody and nothing and I have done nothing in my own might. I am a child of the one and only, true and living God that loves me so much. He decided to use me as an example, and I thank Him for it. It is nothing that I have done because His word says He will use a donkey if He must.

But He does it because He loves. He loves those that He created.

I pray that if anything in here touches you to decide to make the choice to release, to heal and just become free, you move on it. I found out it's the decision that I had to make. Nothing fancy. Just a decision. No one could choose it for me. No one could make it for me. I had to make the decision to trust God and move. No questioning. Just go. Believe His word and go. If He did it for me, He'll do the same for you. He said try Me. And He means it. Try Him. He will never leave you nor forsake you. And He's not a man that He shall lie. Try Him for yourself.

Released to Healing

What God has told you may not be release but the first steps are the same.

Trust, Obey, Act

Release yourself to ......

It took a pandemic, a total shutdown, for me to slow down and stop to hear the voice of God. What will it take for you to hear the word(s) He has just for you?
Can you wait until the next pandemic, or will you take time now to sit and listen for His voice

"I am enough." Says God.

"Stop looking to others for validation.
I have told you who you are. Why do you not
believe Me?
You have trusted Me in so many situations.
You believed in Me for great miracles.
You came to Me for movement in a plethora of
situations.
YET
You do not believe that I mean what I say
regarding your worth.
No man (human) can ever love you the way you
think you need them to until you understand
how valuable you really are.
I have not called you to be accepted by just
some [any] man.
I have not placed you on this earth for the sole
purpose of being a mate for some man.
Know your purpose.
Your purpose is in Me.
Stop looking to a man.
Lift your head and walk towards Me.
I will fill you with every loving word you need
to hear.
I have already written your path in My word.
Stop seeking the attention and accepting what
appears to be affections from man.
Seek first the Kingdom of God."

I must know my worth to God. That's where I will find my fulfillment, joy, peace, love, and happiness.

Tati had the scooter and Kobe had the bike when they went outside. From inside the house, I heard: "Let me see your scooter."

Then I heard what sounded like the scooter bang up against the pavement followed by a crash, like metal hitting a wall.

A voice from a child that I did not recognize said, "You almost ran into that man!"

Another child's voice that I did not recognize followed with, "See if you can jump it!"

At that moment, Tati came in the house looking for Kobe.
She said, "I have his bike. He has my scooter. I don't know where he is, but I want to switch back. I want my scooter."

I then realized that Kobe allowed someone else to use Tatiana scooter without her permission. Whoever had her scooter was not treating it as she would.

My disappointment:
Why would you give something you value away to someone else, free for their use?
1. Did you give them rules and boundaries?
2. Did they give you a covenant investment? What are they giving to you (sacrifice) in exchange for what you are giving to them?

3. Do they know and have they experienced your treatment of the item? They can't understand an expectation they have not experienced.
4. Do they appreciate your cost, your sacrifice to get the item?

No one will treat what you hold valuable like you do.

The value to them is not the same as the value to you.

Your sacrifice for ownership is far more than what they can imagine.

If they misuse it, they don't mind giving it back broken or continuing to use it broken until it is all used up.

God, said:

"Heed to these words, Patrice. I bought you with the ultimate price. You are my child. You can stop someone from mistreating my property. You, my daughter, are valuable and are worthy. You, my daughter, are so broken. You, my daughter, are looking for someone else to care for you the only way I can because I paid for you. You are giving yourself to those who have not made a true covenant/investment with you.

STOP

Know your worth.
Teach Tatiana by your example, not by your words. DO THIS for her investment in herself. Appreciate your cost."

Then these words I heard with so much clarity:
Release
Growth
Sacrifice
Peace
Hope
Reliance
Trust
Promises
Joy
Love
MOVING FORWARD! PRESS ON! MOVE!
FAITH! VICTORY!

You cannot get to NEXT focusing on now.
Although the beginning in both words is "N", the remainder changes.
From 3 letters to 4 letters.
> Something to be gained in the NEXT.
> Something to be learned in the NEXT.
> Something that is valuable in the NEXT.

NEXT, unlike, now, does not contain NO.
> NEXT is full of possibilities.
> NEXT does not definitely, without a doubt, say "no."
> NEXT is not going in circles.
> The "o" is now "e". The vowel has changed and so will I.
> The second step in the NEXT is a change and transformation of something from the now.

NEXT contains a crossroads found in the X.
> A decision must be made to go.
> Directions will shift.
> Something must occur/happen that's different than before.

Jesus is there with me in my NEXT. (Remember it has a "t").
> He will never leave me or forsake me.
> He resides in the next.
> He carries the weight.
> There is no completion without Him.

Don't move ahead of God.
Follow each step to the letter.
If he gives no more, STOP.
Be anxious for nothing.
God has not forgotten me.
He will not abandon me.
Wait for the next direction.

"Release" was given.
      I felt a weight lifted.
"Talk now" was given.
      It was received without argument.
Now NOTHING.
Stop. And wait.

Everything will fall into place when God directs
it.

I MUST ALLOW HIM TO DIRECT.

I pour it out to You, oh Lord.
I break my box of praise.
I break my box of oil.
I break my box of worship.
I pour it out to You, oh Lord.

Good morning, Lord. What a blessing to be here in this place. I cried out to You to get me away from all the distractions, to help me focus on You, to help me calm down so I would not be quick to get angry. You answered with this beautiful little place on Cocoa Beach. If I ask, You will answer.

I must learn that all Your answers may not come swiftly. I must be OK when Your answer is "not yet" or even "no." I must know that You will only do what is best for me.

My Take-Aways from Today's Devotion:
Time to be brave enough to start something new. Lord, give me the courage to step outside of what is safe and comfortable, as I trust You to cover me with Your all-sufficient grace.

GROW MY CAPACITY TO HANDLE LIFE CHALLENGES FROM A POSTURE OF TRUST AND EXPECTATION OF GOOD.

My Take-Aways from A Podcast:
God uses different strategies for different situations. That's why you cannot rely on yesterday's strategy for today's problem, period. God had a reason for wanting you to do things a certain way yesterday....

But....

This is a new day,
So, I need a fresh word from God today.

God resides in the praises of His people.

Psalms 22:1-3 "My God, my God. Why have you forsaken me? Why are you so far from helping me, and from the words of my groaning? Oh my God, I call out by day, but you do not answer; And by night, but I find no rest nor quiet. But you are holy, oh, you who are enthroned in [The holy place where] The praises of Israel [are offered]."

Isaiah 60:18-20 "Violence will not be heard again in your land, nor devastation or destruction within your borders; But you will call your walls salvation, and your gates praise [to God]. The sun will no longer be your light by day, nor shall the bright glow of the moon give light to you, But the Lord will be an everlasting light, for you; And your God will be your glory and splendor. Your son will no longer set, nor will your moon wane; For the Lord will be your everlasting light, and the days of your morning will be over."

Why is it so hard to give up those things which have no nutritional value?

They taste good.

They look good.

BUT they add no value to your diet.

November 27, 2020

Today...my God! What a day!
Today was filled with actions stemming out of emotions.

Hurt, guilt, betrayal, pain, ashamed, shock, brokenness.

God, I ask You remove these things from me and from my husband. Remove them also from my children. Cover them tonight. Let them not hold on to any anger, hurt, animosity, or fear. God protect them from any spiritual attacks. Let nothing but Your love be planted in their minds. I come against depression, self-inflicted pain, thoughts of being alone, thoughts of anger. I come against demonic spirits that have crept in through the doorways that were opened today. I command those spirits to be cast out in the name of Jesus. Cast into void, dark, and dry places not to return. And I call the doorways to be opened no more. Close and seal the doorways so that no little thing that is against the word of God gets in.

Help me, Father, learn of Your love. Help me see and witness Your true love. Just You and me. Take me to next, oh God.

I have stepped out on faith. I have done what I have been so afraid to do. Now Lord, I ask that you take full control. Order my steps, Lord. Control what needs to be controlled so that I

may have favor, and everything works in Your timing and for Your good.
I love You, Father.

My Take-Away's from Today's Devotional:
Get into a rhythm of evaluating and self-reflecting on what's working best, what I want to do next, what skills I need to develop, what connections are required and what would be a small win for me.

I have been set FREE.

Seeing PAIN as a GIFT.
How do I handle the beautiful black box of pain?
If it had not come, I would not be where I am now.

Genesis 45:6-8
"For the famine has been in the land these two years, and there are still five more years in which there will be no plowing and harvesting. God sent me [to Egypt] Ahead of you, to preserve for you a remnant on the earth, and to keep you alive by a great escape. So now. It was not you who sent me here, but God; And he has made me a father to Pharaoh, and Lord of all his household, and ruler over all the land of Egypt."

My PAIN could be my greatest gift.
> Sometimes situations must happen in my life for me to get to my purpose. It gets me to position for God to use me.

This has happened for a reason, because this thing is going to put me in a place where I must do whatever I need to do to pivot and go into a different direction.
> Different meaning new.
> Different meaning my purpose.

I thank God for all the people and situations that have caused me pain.

They were gifts that I never wanted and did not ask to receive but appreciate because of their value.

I thank these people in these situations for playing their role. God has already written and directed my entire life. Everyone must play their part... and play it to perfection they did. God cast every person in my life to play in every situation so that I could walk in purpose, and I thank Him for that.

My self-care is mine.

It does not have to look like anyone else's.
It does not have to fit in a perfectly wrapped
box.

Intentionality

I like walking. Morning or evening.
I like sunsets and sunrises.
I like walking on the beach.
I like podcasts.
I like quiet.

December 28, 2020

God can change MY MESS in 1 DAY.

God has the POWER to change a situation in an instant.

2 Kings 6:33 – 7:2 (NLT)
"While Elisha was still saying this, the messenger arrived. And the king said, "All this misery is from the Lord! Why should I wait for the Lord any longer?" Elisha replied, "Listen to this message from the Lord! This is what the Lord says: By this time tomorrow in the markets of Samaria, six quarts of choice flour will cost only one piece of silver, and twelve quarts of barley grain will cost only one piece of silver." The officer assisting the king said to the man of God, "That couldn't happen even if the lord opened the windows of heaven" But Elisha replied, "You will see it happen with your own eyes, but you won't be able to eat any of it!"

Don't doubt what God Can Do.

Retrain my mind.

Repetition until learning
takes place.

Prepare for the next

I asked God to help me describe what I sometimes experience in my mind and/or body. This can happen suddenly or when someone tells me about a situation, circumstance, or pain they are experiencing.

1) I immediately feel that I know the outcome and I hear myself speaking it in my mind, or
2) I don't know the outcome and immediately, I pray.

But... It doesn't end there.

An all-out battle begins in my mind.

A "What If?" Battle.

It takes me on a type of roller coaster ride. Ok here it is:

I start on the uptake.
> Speaking God's words first.
Then a quick decline.
> But what if?
Turn a corner.
> It may cause this...
Then back on the uptake.
> But God's word says.
By the end of the ride
> I attempt to trust in God. I have spoken and believe the word of God. So why is it so hard to just trust what His word says?
BUT my body is stuck recovering from the ride.

It's like the person whose body makes them queasy after a roller coaster ride, as soon as they regurgitate, they are on to the next ride.

After I take this mental roller coaster ride, my body feels the need to regurgitate the bad and I don't know how to make it. This process turns into a negative event (usually an upset stomach which leads to hospitalization), which requires medication to dissolve the bad or not even dissolve it but to cover up the bad.

Lord, I want to learn to either:
1) Don't go on the ride and STOP at just speaking God's word and believing (trusting) wholeheartedly.
2) Once the ride is over, regurgitate the bad, walk away, and keep enjoying life.

I know God's word and believe it.

I trust what he says to be true.

I go through this battle, Lord. I believe I have on my full armor, but I require help with the following:

Ephesians 6:13 (NLT)
Therefore, put on every piece of God's armor so you will be able to resist the enemy in the time of evil. Then after the battle, you will be standing firm.

Ephesians 6: 15 (NLT)
For shoes, put on the peace that comes from the good news, so that you will be fully prepared.

Ephesians 6: 19 (NLT)
And pray for me, too. Ask God to give me the right words so I can boldly explain God's mysterious plan that the good news is for Jews and Gentiles alike.

Lord help me trust Your word, resist the enemy, stand firm after the battle, and put on peace.

Please Lord, I pray.

Psalm 27:1
King James Version
The Lord is my light and my salvation; whom shall I fear? The Lord is the strength of my life; of whom shall I be afraid?

Amplified Version
The Lord is my light and my salvation - whom shall I fear? The Lord is the refuge and fortress of my life - whom shall I dread?

The Message Version
Light, space, zest - That's God! So with him on my side I am fearless, afraid of no one and nothing.

I must get that part.
I will go through.
Others will go through.
Do not be fearful.
Take refuge in what God says and who God is.

Daniel 3:17-18 (NIV)
If we are thrown into the blazing furnace, the God we serve is able to deliver us from it, and He will deliver us from Your Majesty's hand. But even if He does not, we want you to know, Your Majesty, that we will not serve your gods or worship the image of gold you have set up.

My God is more than able, so I will not give in to fear.

So, I questioned my ability and my belief.
I even compared what someone else was able to do with what I was not able to do.
God is showing me, It's not me.
In me, there is no power, no strength, no fight, no ability.

It is when I give it all to Him.
It is when I stop trying to do the work for Him.
It is when I fully walk in faith, leaning, relying, and depending on only Him and His word.

I must walk expecting to see the finished work as He has told me.

This is my strength: Where I am weak, He is strong.

He allowed situations so that He can show Himself strong and a God of His word. That means I must be made weak.

Trials and tribulations.
Hills and valleys.
Palms and Willows.

They are all pruning to prepare for purpose. My purpose which is in me. My purpose which is not for anyone else or look like anyone else's. It is uniquely given to me because He, The Father, My Father, knows who He created me to be.

I must take time to know (personal, up close) my God. Instead of taking time to know this world and to be entertained by the things of the world which will try to lure me away from Him.

How far am I willing to go for the sake of Christ?
Who am I doing everything for?

Proverbs 27:21(NLT)
Fire tests the purity of silver and gold, but a person is tested being praised.

Am I doing it for God or secretly doing it for me?
Is it about furthering the Kingdom of God?
Recognition is a powerful drug.

Listening to an audible devotional:
"Even though Eve knew truth, she wasn't firmly grounded in truth. She knew what God said, but never fully grasped who He was - completely trustworthy and good."

Why do I get sucked into listening to the strangers lies?
I entertain the enemies lies through my own entertainment.

John 10:1-11 (NLT)
I tell you the truth, anyone who sneaks over the wall of a sheepfold, rather than going through the gate, must surely be a thief and a robber! But the one who enters through the gate is the shepherd of the sheep. The gatekeeper opens the gate for him, and the sheep recognized his voice and come to him. He calls his own sheep by name and leads them out. After he has gathered his own flock, he walks ahead of them, and they follow him because they know his voice. They won't follow a stranger; They will run from him because they don't know his voice." Those who heard Jesus used this illustration didn't understand what he meant, so he explained it to them: "I tell you the truth, I am the gate for

the sheep. All who came before me were thieves and robbers. But the true sheep did not listen to them. Yes, I am the gate. Those who come in through me will be saved. They will come and go freely and will find good pastures. The thief 's purpose is to steal and kill and destroy. My purpose is to give them a rich and satisfying life. I am the Good Shepherd. The Good Shepherd sacrifices his life for the sheep."

Genesis 3:1-5 (AMP)
Now the serpent was more crafty (subtle, skilled in deceit) than any living creature of the field which the Lord God had made. And the serpent Satan said to the woman, "Can it really be that God has said, 'You shall not eat from any tree of the garden'?"
And the woman said to the serpent, "We may eat fruit from the trees of the garden, except the fruit from the tree which is in the middle of the garden. God said, 'You should not eat from it, nor touch it, otherwise you will die'." But the serpent said to the woman, "You certainly will not die. For God knows that on the day you eat from it, your eyes will be opened [that is, you will have greater awareness], and you will be like God, knowing the difference between good and evil."

I must take time to know (personal, up close) my God. Instead of taking time to know this world. And to be entertained by the things of the world which will lure me in and lead me to question the knowledge I have of God.

KNOW MORE ABOUT HIM AND LESS ABOUT THEM.

Them includes:
All those reality shows that do not exemplify the Kingdom of God. Boy, I am so hooked. It's like I'm chained and held captive. Yes that "false reality" world that I am drawn to. I break the chains in the name of Jesus! I am free from "false reality" and take my place in the Kingdom of God.

Retrain - I must replace what I want to reject with what is true and in the word of God.

How? - Study, time, repetition, reading, learning daily.

Whatever God is allowing to be thrown at me, it is for my eternal purpose.
To move me from here to that purpose.

From my devotion:
God unclutter my mind. Untangle my soul from anxiety. Dance my cares away with me. Only You, Lord, cause my spirit to smile.

No path is beyond the scope of God's radar.
Although the path may not have gone the way I would like, God is the Way Maker.

Trust beyond the scope of my perspective.

Beyond what my eyes can see.

Beyond what my mind can even fathom.

Let it go!
Stop holding on to seasonal items.
If you have moved into a new season, why are you still holding on to things of the old season?

Notice the signs that the season is over.

Clean out my closets.

If it is broken, give it completely to the only One who can fix it. This requires me to let it go.

Walking in who God says I am gives me authority to negate, end, and disrupt whatever and/or whoever tries to make me feel contrary. I must recognize the spirit. Bind it and cast it out. I must not allow it to take hold of me.

Important:
Recognize what is in me that keeps me running back holding on to stuff and/or people that I am not supposed to bring with me in the new season.

FIND IT, RECOGNIZE IT, BIND IT, MOVE FORWARD.

<u>Podcast – Notes and Thoughts</u>
- Have an offensive, not defensive, prayer life.
- Be quiet if I am not saying what God is saying.
- Surrender constantly. Safeguard my surrender. Body, mouth, mind, business work.
  > Safeguard means remove things that feed my worldly desires.
- Unfollow people who would trigger things in me. This means I must pay attention to how I respond.
- Separate myself from people, places, and things that distort biblical principles.
- I must have tunnel vision about God and His plan for my life. Focused on God.
- Frustration in a moment will cause me to make mistakes that will blow it for me.

I don't want to blow it.

The more I grow, the more that is at stake.

- Must use what I have learned in previous seasons.

I want to go from Glory to Glory, Faith to Faith.

What that means is I want more of You, Lord.
I want to know You in a closer, more intimate way.
I want to be with You, in Your presence, at all times.
I want to be consumed with You.
I want my thoughts to be Your thoughts.
I want my ways to be Your ways.
I want to fully, without any reservation, trust the plans You have for me and trust that they are good.
I want to not question the process but draw closer to You through the process.
I cannot allow my emotions and feelings get me stuck in the process.

GROWTH AT ALL TIMES.

Just not sprouting quickly but getting all the nourishment I need to be strong both internally and externally to have such an intricate, detailed, strong holding rooting system that nothing would stop me from being continuously focused on You.

Trials come to make me stronger.
Growth through the trials.
Lessons in the trials.
These are steps from Glory to Glory.

God promised me peace.
Wait for it. It will come.
Stop trying to find it in someone or something.
Totally live for God in all things, with all things.

ONLY GOD CAN GIVE ME THAT WHICH I LACK.

HE HAS IT ALL.

"A weekend full of amusements and fun? Such common remedies might offer temporary relief from stress, but the long term, ongoing answer for anxiety is simple prayer pouring out your heart to God. Linger in prayer to find out His perspective."

God's peace will guard my heart and mind.

From my February 6, 2021, entry:
If it doesn't help me grow, walk away from it.

Growth has many forms.
I need to determine what I like or don't like.
What I will accept or will not accept.
What matters to me.

Does my desire to be wanted outweigh my desire to grow?

My growth must always be in the
direction of God.

You don't always have to speak your truth, especially when it may hurt someone else. Why is there a need to have someone else validate or even listen to your perspective? What is needed is to validate and hear the other person. I must be willing to listen, value, learn, adjust, and change.

The same methods will not give different results. 2 + 2 will always be 4. If I want to change the result, I must add to or subtract something from the equation itself. That equation is controlled by me. The result is predetermined by God. To change the result to something I want, I must choose carefully and not haphazardly. My choice is a process or should be a process that is well thought out and compared to God's word.

$$2 + 2 + (\quad) - (\quad) = 10$$

(I must carefully choose. Although there are many answers that will work, only one is the one the teacher is looking for. The great thing about this is the teacher gives me the answer, I just have to sit and listen.)

Teach me to sit and listen instead of always being ready to validate my responses and choices.

Don't allow anyone to direct my path. Be directed by God and only God.

Why do I continue to search for what I already have?

Why do I look at others for what they have?
Why Covet?
Why jealousy?
When will I realize I have everything that belongs to My Father. I have it in Him and through Him. All my needs, desires, and wants He will provide.

March 20, 2021

I am wonderfully and fearfully made.
God made me who I am, and that is in His image and likeness.
God loves me for me because He knew me before I was born.
Every part of me, God created for good, and it is good because God said so.
It doesn't matter what man believes, thinks, or assumes.
I am made special for the Kingdom by the Creator of the Kingdom.

I am confident.
I am secure.
I am beautiful.
I am worth love.
I am worthy of joy and happiness.

No man can take my value away from me.
I will not allow it.

I am not to be played with.
I am not to be used.
I am not to be abused.
I am not to be manipulated.

I am a child of The King.
I am to be treated as such, and I deserve to be treated as the daughter of the Creator of the universe.

I am finding that there will be days when I miss companionship. I miss having a person around to laugh with, talk to, to hug, cuddle, and lay down beside me.

God, I ask that I learn to go to You. God, You are my companion. I want to have a conversation with You. I want to laugh from the joy You give me.

I know it is not the same as a human, but I also know that You can fulfill me far beyond any man.

Lord. Let me desire You over the attention of a man. Let me commune with You. Teach me to call out for You instead of texting and calling out for a man.

April 4, 2021

I control nothing.

Even my decisions and choices I give to You, Lord. On this journey and in this season, I am learning to totally depend on You and have full faith in Your word. My courage and strength come from You. My joy and peace are within You. I thank You for all that You've allowed.

I went across the Selman Expressway. Nervous, but You said You got me so I can go. And I went.
I got on a small plane. Nervous, but You said You got me. So, I went.
I got a divorce. Nervous, but said I knew I heard from You and You said You got me. So, I went.
I moved into my own place. Nervous and scared, but You said You got me.

SO I WENT, MOVED.
AND I AM HERE.

You are my solid rock.
I can lean on You, and You won't move.
Thank You, Jesus.
I love You.
You keep showing up and providing my needs. I know You are always with me.
Obedience is my repayment to You. Obedience is my worship.

Heal my heart, Oh God!
I want to run after You, not another man.
Stop the pain of abandonment.
Heal the brokenness I feel about myself.
Help me overcome thoughts of worthlessness and the idea that I am not enough.
Help me love myself so that I can completely love others.
Help me understand that I am enough, more than enough.

For I know what You have called me, so help me walk in it daily.

I cannot allow my thoughts to outweigh Your word.

I am worthy of love.
I am worthy of the best.
I am worthy of affection.

I am a good woman and I must understand that I should be sought after.

"He who finds..."

I chase only after You from this point forward.
I align my heart to Your heart.
I will seek Your face.
I will praise Your name.
I will worship You with my life.
Not seeking man.
You have all I need.

Lord, lead the way.
I follow

Lord, I have conflicting feelings.

I don't want those who have hurt me to be hurt. I pray that they prosper, and I don't want anyone to think badly of them.

Maybe I stay quiet.
Maybe I keep protecting them.

Then Lord. I can't tell my testimony.
Then my testimony can't be used for Your glory.

God, I am conflicted.

Can I heal from what I experienced without truly acknowledging what I experienced?
How do You get the glory from all of this if I don't tell my story?
How can I say that my life is not my own meanwhile, I'm protecting it and treating it as if it only belongs to me?
Am I thinking more of these people than I am of You?

This is my spiritual and human (mind) battle.
Conflicted.
This is really hard.

I want more of you, Lord. For that to happen, I must be emptied of me. For that to happen, I must recognize what is in me so that I can take the appropriate steps to empty it. Get rid of it.

I see hurt.
I see unforgiveness.
I see resentment.
I see brokenness.
I see self-doubt.
I see false humility.
I see pride.

I want to turn to you.
I want to be accountable to your word.
Help me.

My flesh is weak.
Sometimes, many times it's hard not to give in.
Help me.

Satan, the blood of Jesus is against you.
I am victorious.
I am a child of God.
The battle was already won.
Satan, you are defeated.
Christ lives in me.
The same Christ that defeated you.
Thank you, Holy Spirit for the reminder.
I want more of you, Lord.

Today, my father told me for the first time, that he knows he is dying, and these are his final days. He told me that doctors are trying to help him manage the pain until he passes.

Radiation every day for three weeks to manage pain.

Pain medicines almost every two to three hours to manage pain.

New procedure to manage pain.

He said at this point nothing will stop it and nothing will help.

Writing is my way of prayer and turning this thing over to You, Lord.

Make me righteous before You.
Purify me.

I want to make you smile, oh God.
I want to live for You.
I desire for You to pour into me, so that I may pour into others.

Anything that is not like You, God, strip me and cleanse me from it.

Control my flesh.
I do not want to sin against You.

How much life am I pouring into myself? Am I speaking into myself?

I must redefine how I see love.
I was tasked with determining how love should feel, how love should be, what it is and what it is not.

I was told to stop saying I am broken.
I am healed, I am not broken.

I must identify who I am to myself. Who is the real Patrice?

I will be happy with me.
I want to not need others for my happiness so much.
I want to learn how to be my own best friend.
I want to learn how to love me like no other.
I want to learn how to love me like God loves me.
I am worth it.

I am released to my healing!

YES Lord!

After putting this book together, I realized that satan would have loved for me to continue to stay and focus on my bad situation so I would not get to next. The goal was for me to stay in the now so that I would not begin to heal and be able to move into the next.

I am no longer in fear.

I am no longer afraid.

I say YES Lord.

Have Your way!

With all that You have brought me through, I dare not trust You.